**Mr. **

il.

32 pages • 8.5 x 11 • Color illus throughout
includes 5-minute musical audio CD
For children ages 2 - 8 • Science Notes
Parent Teacher Activities • Sheet Music
ISBN: 978-1-933818-13-9
$18.95 laminated hardcover
Publication date: **September 2007**

For additional information, to arrange an
interview with the author and/or illustrator, or to
receive art electronically, please contact:
Kate Bandos, KSB Promotions, **800-304-3269**
or kate@ksbpromotions.com

Published by Animalations™; distribution by Biblio
Distribution. Available from bookstores nationwide, from
online booksellers including amazon.com, by calling
1-877-804-9767 or at www.animalations.com.

Please send two copies of any review or mention to
Animalations™ • 4186 Melodia Songo Court
Las Vegas, NV 89135

M000122194

Mr. Walrus
& the OLD SCHOOL BUS

Patricia Derrick

Mr. Walrus
& the OLD SCHOOL BUS

Illustrated by

J-P Loppo Martinez

We're cruisin' around town
In our old school bus,
But we can't be late
We have a **five** o'clock date.

Mr. Walrus, please,
Go on and drive.
We can't be late...
It's <u>nine</u> forty five.

We're off to the Zoo,
Just me and you.
We're going to see
Bears and snakes,
And **al-li-ga-tors** too.

Now, it's off to the fair
Without a care.
All our friends are already there,
Pop-corn to share.

Mr. Walrus, please,
Go on and drive.
We can't be late...
It's <u>eleven</u> forty five.

To Grandma's house
We like to go.
We always have a really good time...
So don't drive so slow.

I have a hunch
That it's time for lunch...
'Have carrots to crunch
And peanuts to munch.

Make a quick stop
At the ice cream shop...
'Have **choc-o-late** drop
And a cherry on top.

Let's fetch our dog
At the beauty shop...
He had a doggy groom,
He smells like **per-fume**!

Mr. Walrus, please,
Go on and drive.
We can't be late...
It's <u>three</u> forty five.

Let's stop at the store
To help our Mom...
Get milk and bread
From Grocer Tom.

Mr. Walrus, please,
Go on and drive.
We can't be late...
It's <u>four</u> forty five.

Now, we're **fi-nal-ly** home.
And we're just in time
For our dinner date...
"A **spa-ghet-ti** plate."

Mr. Walrus, please,
Go on and drive.
To-mor-row at ten...
Let's try it again!

To-mor-row at ten...
Let's try it again.

Three R's Before Reading

Rhythm • Rhyme • Repetition

Three R's before Reading (Rhythm, Rhyme and Repetition) uses multi-sensory stimulation to fire neurons in the brain. Multi-sensory stimulation creates strong connections between neurons. With strong connections, learning becomes easier.

Rhythm is found in music and movement. Rhythm is experienced when we listen to musical sounds, decipher what is heard and move to the beat. Children will literally get up on their feet and start dancing when they hear "foot tapping" music. Children will want to participate when they hear rhythm. Participation can include everything that makes up a "multi-sensory" experience for the child.

Rhyme: Rhyming verses provide patterns. Patterns are found in poetry, rhyming books and in musical songs. Children love the sound of patterns. They can feel what they hear throughout their bodies. Patterns stimulate the right side of the brain. The right side of the brain is responsible for math and spatial relationships, as well as language.

Repetition: Children love to repeat stimulating experiences over and over again. When children ask to do an activity again, they are really saying, "I want to feel those sensations again." Children feel sensations when the activity is "multi-sensory". If a child is given an opportunity to participate in a multi-sensory book, the child will want to read that particular book over and over again.

Animalations books provide multi-sensory stimulation and make learning easier for children.

Mr. Walrus and the Old School Bus provides opportunities for learning experiences beyond reading a story. Adapt the suggested activities on this page to provide age appropriate learning for all children participating in Mr. Walrus and the Old School Bus.

Movement:

Move chairs together to form the shape of a School Bus. Children will enjoy sitting in the chair "bus seats" and taking turns as Mr. Walrus, the bus driver. Give children an opportunity to express themselves through movement as they participate in Mr. Walrus and the Old School Bus.

Social:

Plan a school bus field trip with various stops around your community. Plan stops at the zoo and the fair and have people waiting there to greet the children. Plan a stop at the local pet shop and grocery store. Be sure to allow plenty of time for lunch, with lots of carrots to crunch.

If the bus stops are in your playground or backyard, use props and signs to designate the various stops. The children will enjoy adding new bus stops to their trip.

Learning to Use Clocks to Tell Time:

As you take your bus trips (either around town or on your imaginary trip), use clocks to tell the time and make sure you are not late for your next bus stop. Children will learn the importance of being on time by using a clock.

Art:

Draw a map of your community and the bus stops you will take on your trip. Help very young children use familiar shapes (squares and circles) to show various bus stops. Glue on animal stickers to finish off the map. Keep in mind that each child will have his or her own interpretation, so no two maps will be alike.

Language:

Allow the children an opportunity to explain their maps to others in the group. Self esteem will "sizzle" as children share their maps with others. Invite children to share their work with family members, friends, and grandparents, as well as post their drawings on home refrigerators to share with others over and over.

Searching:

Look for the red clock that appears on some pages.
Count the number of red clocks in the book.

Science Notes
WALRUS

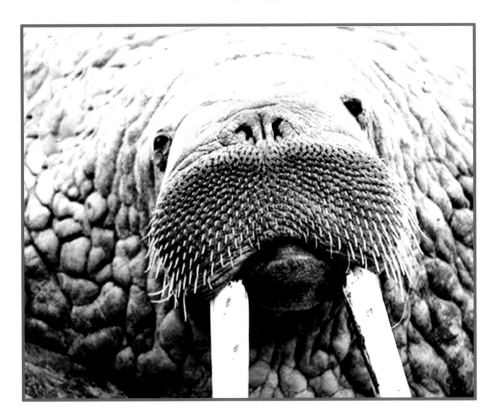

Walrus are red skinned sea mammals that live in cold Alaskan waters. They grow up to 14 feet long and weigh 2,000 pounds. The walrus has a short neck, a mustache, three-foot ivory tusks, and flippers. A walrus nose or snout has about 700 mustache hairs.

Walrus love to sunbathe and swim in cold waters. They can dive as deep as 300 feet. Walrus use their tusks to brace themselves when climbing in and out of water and also to anchor themselves while digging for clams. Walrus like to eat clams, snails, mussels, and other kinds of sea creatures found at the bottom of the ocean.

The walrus has air sacs under his throat that he can fill like a floatation device to bob around in the water. A walrus can move very quickly on land using all four flippers.

The walrus squirts water out of his mouth like a jet stream when he is digging for clams.

This book is dedicated to the animals in our zoos
and zoo keepers who keep them healthy and content.
On behalf of all young visitors, thank you for the
delightful and educational experience.

Patricia Derrick, Author

Master of Education from the University of Utah
Early Childhood and Elementary School Educator
Owner and Operator of Early Learning Schools: 30 years
Assistant Professor, Metropolitan State College, Mesa College Campus, GJ Colorado

Author Patricia Derrick is available for speaking engagements and conferences
Email: info@animalations.com for more information

Mr. Walrus and the Old School Bus

Publishing
4186 Melodia Songo Court
Las Vegas, Nevada 89135

ISBN # 1-933818-13-1
ISBN # 978-1-933818-13-9

Complimentary replacement CD's for libraries:
Send requests to: info@animalations.com

Printed in Korea

Also Available from Animalations:

Farley the Ferret of Farkleberry Farm:
Farley and the farmer take bread and jam to the fair, but when the drought hit Foley County, there was no jam to share. Children danced around the vines and made silent wishes in their minds. Find out what happened to the berries on Farkleberry Farm. Message: Farley and the children found a way to help others.

Riley the Rhinoceros:
Riley is called the jungle bus because he gives rides to baby animals as they find their way back home. But, he can't give rides to all the animals because that would be preposterous.
Message: ...helping others and friendship.

Rickity & Snickity at the Balloon Fiesta:
Two Rocky Mountain cubs hide in the back of the Park Rangers van to attend the Balloon Fiesta. The cubs rode in the hot air balloon with such ease, everyone thought they were celebrities. Join the fun at the Balloon Fiesta. Message: Baby animals grow to their full size very rapidly. Try to imagine bear cubs riding in a hot air balloon.

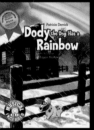

Dody the Dog has a Rainbow:
Dody the dog is lost and travels through the town and countryside looking for his home. Dody eventually finds his rainbow to help him find his way.
Message: There is hope inside your rainbow.

Sly the Dragonfly:
Sly the Dragonfly loves to fly high. "I hear the wind whistling through my wings. It makes my heart wake up and sing". Sly encourages young readers to be the best that they can be.
Message: Life is all about the way you live each day.

Montgomery the Moose:
With five distinct musical styles, Montgomery the Moose shakes his caboose for his friends. Young readers will learn to appreciate different kinds of music and participate in movement activities. Message: If you practice enough, you can accomplish most things you would like to do.